## DISCOVER DOGS WITH THE AMERICAN CANINE ASSOCIATION

# I LIKE SAINT BERNARDS!

Linda Bozzo

It is the mission of the American Canine Association (ACA) to provide registered dog owners with the educational support needed for raising, training, showing, and breeding the healthiest pets expected by responsible pet owners throughout the world. Through our activities and services, we encourage and support the dog world in order to promote best-known husbandry standards as well as to ensure that the voice and needs of our customers are quickly and properly addressed.

Our continued support, commitment, and direction are guided by our customers, including veterinary, legal, and legislative advisors. ACA aims to provide the most efficient, cooperative, and courteous service to our customers and strives to set the standard for education and problem solving for all who depend on our services.

For more information, please visit www.acacanines.com, email customerservice@acadogs.com, phone 1-800-651-8332, or write to the American Canine Association at PO Box 121107, Clermont, FL 34712.

Published in 2019 by Enslow Publishing, LLC.
101 W. 23rd Street, Suite 340, New York, NY 10011

Copyright © 2019 by Enslow Publishing, LLC.

All rights reserved.

No part of this book may be reproduced by any means without the written permission of the publisher.

**Library of Congress Cataloging-in-Publication Data**

Names: Bozzo, Linda, author.
Title: I like Saint Bernards! / Linda Bozzo.
Description: New York, NY : Enslow Publishing, 2019. | Series: Discover dogs with the American Canine Association | Audience: K to Grade 3. | Includes bibliographical references and index.
Identifiers: LCCN 2018008247| ISBN 9781978501928 (library bound) | ISBN 9781978502659 (paperback) | ISBN 9781978502666 (6 pack)
Subjects: LCSH: Saint Bernard dog—Juvenile literature.
Classification: LCC SF429.S3 B69 2019 | DDC 636.73—dc23
LC record available at https://lccn.loc.gov/2018008247

Printed in the United States of America

**To Our Readers:** We have done our best to make sure all websites in this book were active and appropriate when we went to press. However, the author and the publisher have no control over and assume no liability for the material available on those websites or on any websites they may link to. Any comments or suggestions can be sent by email to customerservice@enslow.com.

**Photo Credits:** Cover, pp. 1, 3 (right) tobkatrina/Shutterstock.com; pp. 3 (left), 10 Grigorita Ko/Shutterstock.com; p. 5 Cappi Thompson/Moment/Getty Images; p. 6 Marcel Jancovic/Shutterstock.com; p. 9 THEPALMER/E+/Getty Images; p. 13 (left) Valeriya Popova 22/Shutterstock.com; p 13 (right) graphicphoto/Thinkstock/(collar), Luisa Leal Photography/Shutterstock.com (bed), gvictoria/Shutterstock.com (brush), exopixel/Shutterstock.com (dishes), © iStockphoto.com/Lisa Thornberg (leash, toys); p. 14 © iStockphoto.com/jodiecoston; p. 17 Kev Gregory/Shutterstock.com; p. 18 Purestock/Alamy Stock Photo; p. 19 ItCameWithTheFrame/Shutterstock.com; p. 21 MirasWonderland/Shutterstock.com.

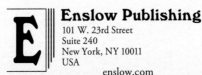

101 W. 23rd Street
Suite 240
New York, NY 10011
USA

enslow.com

# CONTENTS

**IS A SAINT BERNARD RIGHT FOR YOU?** 4

**A DOG OR A PUPPY?** 7

**LOVING YOUR SAINT BERNARD** 8

**EXERCISE** 11

**FEEDING YOUR SAINT BERNARD** 12

**GROOMING** 15

**WHAT YOU SHOULD KNOW** 16

**A GOOD FRIEND** 19

**NOTE TO PARENTS** 20

**WORDS TO KNOW** 22

**READ ABOUT DOGS** 23

**INDEX** 24

# IS A SAINT BERNARD RIGHT FOR YOU?

Saint Bernards are one of the largest dog breeds. They can weigh almost 200 pounds (91 kilograms)! Due to their big size, homes with small children are not best for Saint Bernards.

Everything about the breed is huge, so they need lots of space. If your home has lots of room and no small children, a Saint Bernard may be right for you.

## A DOG OR A PUPPY?

Saint Bernards make great family pets when they are trained. If you do not have time to train a puppy, you may want an older Saint Bernard instead.

*Saint Bernard puppies grow very fast and need to be trained not to jump on people.*

## LOVING YOUR SAINT BERNARD

This dog is friendly, calm, and gentle. He loves to spend time with his family. Show your Saint Bernard love with lots of snuggles.

> They're usually quiet dogs, but they will bark when they have a reason.

## EXERCISE

Saint Bernards don't need much exercise. A romp in a large fenced yard or walks on a leash will keep this dog happy. Your Saint Bernard will likely enjoy a nap after a game of fetch.

Saint Bernards have a great sense of smell.

# FEEDING YOUR SAINT BERNARD

Saint Bernards can be fed wet or dry dog food. Ask a veterinarian (vet), a doctor for animals, which food is best for your dog and how much to feed her.

Give your Saint Bernard fresh, clean water every day.

Remember to keep your dog's food and water dishes clean. Dirty dishes can make a dog sick.

Do not feed your dog people food. It can make her sick.

## Your new dog will need:

a collar with a tag

a bed

a brush

food and water dishes

a leash

toys

# GROOMING

Saint Bernards can shed a lot. This means their hair falls out. There are short-haired and long-haired Saint Bernards. Long-haired dogs need to be brushed more often. They can both be bathed when needed. Make sure you use shampoo made specially for dogs.

Your Saint Bernard's fast-growing nails will need to be clipped. A vet or groomer can show you how. Your dog's ears should be cleaned, and his teeth should be brushed by an adult.

## WHAT YOU SHOULD KNOW

Saint Bernards do not do well in the heat. However, they can handle cold weather.

These giant dogs are messy. They drool and bring mud and dirt into the house.

You will most likely hear your Saint Bernard snore when he sleeps.

This breed was developed by monks in Switzerland to rescue people who got lost in the mountains.

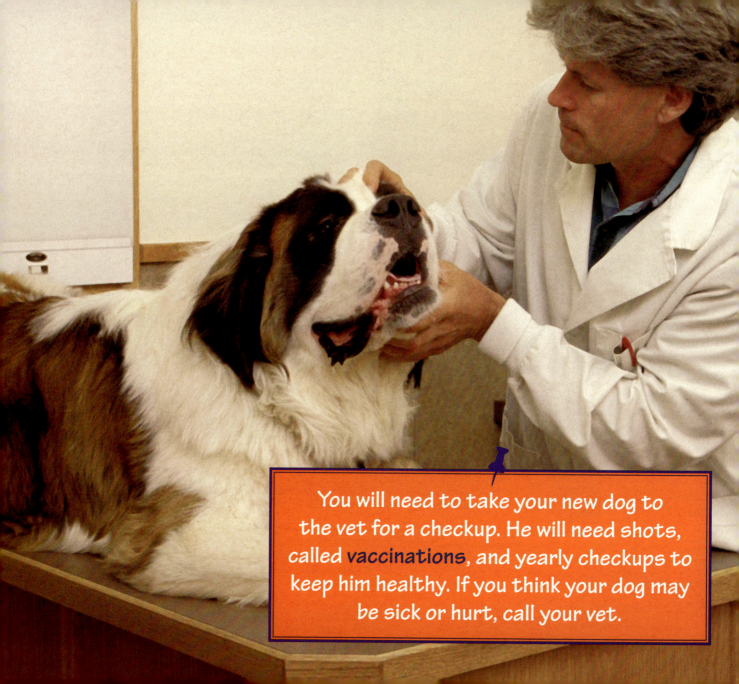

You will need to take your new dog to the vet for a checkup. He will need shots, called **vaccinations**, and yearly checkups to keep him healthy. If you think your dog may be sick or hurt, call your vet.

## A GOOD FRIEND

The Saint Bernard is a loving, quiet dog who protects her family. She will be a good friend for years.

Saint Bernards can live eight to ten years.

## NOTE TO PARENTS

It is important to consider having your dog spayed or neutered when the dog is young. Spaying and neutering are operations that prevent unwanted puppies and can help improve the overall health of your dog.

It is also a good idea to microchip your dog, in case he or she gets lost. A vet will implant a microchip under the skin containing an identification number that can be scanned at a vet's office or animal shelter. The microchip registry is contacted, and the company uses the ID number to look up your information from a database.

Some towns require licenses for dogs, so be sure to check with your town clerk.

For more information, speak with a vet.

There are many dogs, young and old, waiting to be adopted from animal shelters and rescue groups.

## Words to Know

**fetch**  To go after a toy and bring it back.

**groomer**  A person who bathes and brushes dogs.

**leash**  A chain or strap that attaches to the dog's collar.

**monks**  Religious men who live with others like them away from society.

**romp**  Rough play.

**shed**  When a dog's hair falls out so new hair can grow.

**vaccinations**  Shots that dogs need to stay healthy.

**veterinarian (vet)**  A doctor for animals.

## Read About Dogs

## Books

Clapper, Nikki Bruno. *Saint Bernards*. North Mankato, MN: Capstone Press, 2016.

Rustad, Martha. *Saint Bernards*. Mankato, MN: Amicus, 2018.

Sommer, Nathan. *Saint Bernards*. Minneapolis, MN: Bellweather Media, Inc., 2018.

## Websites

**American Canine Association Inc., Kids Corner**
*www.acakids.com*
Visit the official website of the American Canine Association.

**National Geographic for Kids, Pet Central**
*kids.nationalgeographic.com/explore/pet-central*
Learn more about dogs and other pets at the official site of the National Geographic Society for Kids.

# INDEX

**B**
barking, 8
bathing, 15
bed, 13
brush, 13, 15

**C**
children, 4
cold weather, 16
collar, 13

**D**
dishes, 12, 13
drooling, 16

**E**
ears, 15
exercise, 11

**F**
family, 8, 19
fetch, 11
food, 12, 13

**G**
grooming, 15

**H**
hair, 15
heat, 16

**L**
leash, 11, 13
license, 20
life span, 19

**M**
messy, 16
microchipping, 20
monks, 16

**N**
nails, 15
nap, 11

**O**
older dog, 7

**P**
personality, 8, 19
protection, 19
puppy, 7, 20

**R**
romp, 11

**S**
shedding, 15
size, 4, 16
smell, sense of, 11
snoring, 16
spay/neuter, 20
Switzerland, 16

**T**
tags, 13
teeth, 15
toys, 13

**V**
vaccinations, 18
veterinarian, 12, 18, 20

**W**
walking, 11
water, 12, 13